NORMAL

Katie Pollock

CURRENCY PRESS
The performing arts publisher

CURRENT THEATRE SERIES

First published in 2019
by Currency Press Pty Ltd,
PO Box 2287, Strawberry Hills, NSW, 2012, Australia
enquiries@currency.com.au
www.currency.com.au

in association with The Uncertainty Principle.

Typeset by Dean Nottle for Currency Press.
Cover by Madison Avenue x Manifold.

Currency Press acknowledges the Traditional Owners of the Country on which we live and work. We pay our respects to all Aboriginal and Torres Strait Islander Elders, past and present.

A catalogue record for this book is available from the National Library of Australia

Contents

WRITER'S NOTE

Normal was inspired by the true story of eighteen teenage girls who were struck down by a Tourette's-like illness in the small town of Le Roy, in upstate New York. The girls' illness was blamed on environmental toxins, or a psychological disorder, or drugs, or social media, or vaccines, or any number of other evils. The media descended and paralysed the town.

I was lucky enough to receive the Edward Albee/Inscription Playwriting Scholarship during the writing of this play, which allowed me to travel to New York and Le Roy to research the story. I stayed in the town and talked to anyone who would talk to me about what had happened. I had a long and interesting interview with the editor of the local newspaper, the *Batavian*, about how the whole saga had played out. I even got a terrible haircut so I could get the gossip at the local hairdressers. They blamed a party drug known as bath salts. The waitresses in the diner said it was all fake. The lady in the antiques shop said it was because the Jello factory had closed down and there were no jobs left. The *Batavian* editor was more interested in a political cover-up than the cause.

But *Normal* is not about those events, fascinating as they are. For this play, I wanted to lift the story out of the realm of reality, and away from its American context, and place it in a metaphorical space.

I was interested in both the concept of 'normality/difference' and the phenomenon of mass psychogenic illness—more commonly called mass hysteria—especially its associations with young women. The phenomenon usually arises in small or close-knit communities where the opinions of those around you are vital to survival and acceptance—small towns and villages, religious communities, schools, extended families—places where the social membrane is very tightly drawn.

Historically the diagnosis of hysteria has been used as a way to silence 'troublesome' women—those who upset the social order—through its negative connotations. It's a diagnosis that has been used by men against women, young women in particular, for a very long time. Because after you've called them hysteric you don't have to delve any deeper into what's actually going on in their lives—especially if they are not able to verbalise it themselves.

The literary critic Elaine Showalter talks of hysteria as a 'protolanguage', a body language for people who otherwise might not be able to speak or otherwise express what they feel. She renames stories of hysteria, with all their tropes passed down through culture and myth, as 'hystories'.

The most famous of these of course is *The Crucible* by Arthur Miller. This play is in no way an attempt to retell Miller's story. But there is a conversation with the literary conventions he uses, particularly with his depiction of Abigail as a villain. In *Normal*, Poppy is our protagonist and the story is told from her perspective—a female point of view. I've tried to work against some of the literary stereotypes by showing her not as either/or, villain or victim, but something more human, more in-between.

So, is she 'normal'? The idea of normal is so ordinary, yet it's also restrictive and repressive. Life can be very hard when you're young and working out who you are, especially when you don't have role models for difference. We don't handle difference very well as a society and many of us try and squeeze ourselves into the wrong shape. Even when we self-declare as freaks, geeks and weirdos, we're still defining ourselves in opposition to this mythical force of normality.

So this is Poppy's journey and her struggle, as it is for many of us—to work out what she is and where she fits, and how to live in a way that feels true to herself.

Katie Pollock

Normal was first produced by The Uncertainty Principle at The Old 505 Theatre, Sydney, on 29 May 2019, with the following cast:

SHOP GIRL / MS HOLT / LUCY / ENSEMBLE	Chika Ikogwe
POPPY	Alexandra Morgan
HEATHER / SASHA / ENSEMBLE	Cecilia Morrow
SKY / SHEILA / ENSEMBLE	Finley Penrose

Director, Anthony Skuse
Assistant Director, Olivia Aleksoski
Lighting and Set Designer, Kelsey Lee
Sound Designer, Cluny Edwards
Stage Manager, Gundega Lapsa
Assistant Producer, James Balian

CHARACTERS

POPPY WILLIAMS, teenage girl

SKY, Poppy's best friend

HEATHER, Poppy's mum

SHOP GIRL, a shop girl

MS HOLT, school principal

SHEILA HARRINGTON, psychiatrist

SASHA, Poppy's friend-ish

LUCY PORTER, mother of Sasha

REPORTER

DOCTORS

In the first production of the play, one actor played Poppy and three actors shared the other roles. The director may choose to cast one actor per role, or to work with any other combination.

NOTE: The author strongly encourages the producer to collaborate with artists from diverse backgrounds in the realisation and presentation of this work.

SETTING

A small town.

The action should slide and jump between various places. No set pieces.

NOTES

Some of the girls' physical and phonic tics are scripted and some are not—these are not set in stone. In rehearsal and performance, the tics and their level and frequency are to be worked out between the actors and director. The phonic tic 'nuh nuh nuh' is indicative for the actor or reader, not prescriptive. Physical tics are written in stage directions as *[tic]* indicating they are suggestions only. Directions not in square brackets should be treated as regular stage directions.

Where there is a dash (—) in place of a character name, the line is to be played by a member of the ensemble. Where there is a dash after a character name, the actor should take the moment.

This play has been developed with the assistance of the Inscription/ Edward Albee Playwriting Scholarship, the Australian Writers' Guild, and the inaugural Ingenious Grant from Town Hall Theater, MA (USA).

This project has been assisted by the Australian Government through the Australia Council for the Arts, its arts funding and advisory body.

This play went to press before the end of rehearsals and may differ from the play as performed.

SCENE ONE

POPPY: I think it was there
somewhere inside—
at least some nano part of it.
A flicker
or
like a shadow before the sun comes out instead of after.
But not
not this—
[tic]
Shit.
Sorry.
[tic, tic, tic]
You know when you're a kid and you have a cold and you don't
want to blow
[tic]
blow your nose so you just—

> *She blows short bursts through her nose.*

That was me.
Always me.
But don't all kids
[tic]
do that?
Now it's like sparks going off in my head
[tic]
and I
[tic]
I can't put them out.
[tic, tic]
I don't know how it turned into this whole other—
why it got this bad.
I don't know why the others have it.
Ask them.
[tic, blink, blink]

You'll have to ask them.

…

Stop looking at me

[tic, tic]

like I'm a freak.

I already know I am.

SCENE TWO

Earlier. Before POPPY *has any tics.*

Sky's house. Music. POPPY *and* SKY *dance together.*

POPPY: This one. Sky, Sky, this one.

SKY: Oh, I love this! Do you love this?

POPPY: Come on! Bring it!

> *They dance.*
>
> *Sky's phone pings.*
>
> SKY *puts it away without answering.*

Sex talk or bitch talk?

SKY: Neither.

POPPY: Let me see.

SKY: Nuh.

POPPY: Must be sex.

SKY: Is not. Shut up, okay.

POPPY: Ooh! Something sexy you want to hide from me.

SKY: It's nothing. Just ignore it.

POPPY: Someone you actually like maybe?

SKY: It's not even anybody.

POPPY: Are you sure?

SKY: Oh god, will you shut up? You're killing my vibe.

> *They dance.*

POPPY: Ohmygod, awesome move.

SKY: I know.

POPPY: That looks so cool the way you—

SKY: I know, right?

> *More excellent dancing.*

Sky's phone pings again.

SKY *ignores it.*

POPPY: Someone wants you.

SKY: I said shut up.

POPPY: I need to see this.

POPPY *grabs Sky's phone.*

SKY: Hey!

POPPY: Seriously? Your mum messages you from downstairs?

SKY: Totally nothing, see?

POPPY: Mine just yells.

SKY: Too many stairs.

POPPY: [*reading the text*] Tutor is here? So, what, you randomly have a tutor now? Since when?

SKY: Dumb waste of time.

POPPY: You failed maths, right?

SKY: The whole thing is stupid.

POPPY: Okay, random question: What are the three consecutive integers that add up to six?

SKY: Dumb, dumber and who cares?

POPPY: Wow. You're so right. You don't need a tutor at all.

SKY: Dad wants to send me to Grammar.

POPPY: What?!

SKY: So now I have to pass their stupid exam.

POPPY: Just like that? Why?

SKY: He says Mum's socialist flirtation with the public system has failed 'as predicted' and it's time I got a proper education before it's too late.

POPPY: No! You can't go to Grammar!

SKY: I know, right?

POPPY: What about me?

SKY: I know.

POPPY: Who am I going to hang on the field with?

SKY: Exactly.

POPPY: I'll be totally on my own.

SKY: Yeah. Apart from everyone else.

POPPY: Who?

SKY: Ashley, Paris, Bronte …

POPPY: APB out for crimes against intelligence, Sky. Nothing going on behind the eyeliner.

SKY: You'll still have Sasha.

POPPY: Okay, I have Sasha. But what about us? We're the girls! We're the team! We're the legends!

SKY: The legends!

POPPY: Right?

SKY: It's not like I wanna go.

POPPY: So tell him.

SKY: He keeps going, 'It's normal to want the best for your children'.

POPPY: Seriously? Blazer and long socks? That is so not normal.

Sky's phone pings again.

SKY: Coming!

POPPY: Just tell your dad you're not going. Tell him you want to stay with your friends.

SKY: Yeah, right.

POPPY: This sucks.

SKY: Although I'll totally smash those Grammar bitches in cool.

POPPY: What?

SKY: I'll be giving them, like, lessons in badass.

POPPY: But what about us?

SKY: I know, alright?

POPPY: No, I mean like, you and me?

POPPY *tries to take* SKY's *hand.* SKY *pulls away.*

SKY: Anyway, I'm still going to Sasha's party. It's not like Dad's banned me from life.

POPPY: She's talking it up like it's this huge deal. I mean, it'll probably be totally lame.

SKY: Want to see my outfit? It's hot as.

POPPY: God, I have nothing to wear. I seriously look like a troll in everything I own.

SKY: So get something new.

POPPY: I dunno. I can't.

SKY: How come?

POPPY: It's complicated.

SKY: How is shopping complicated? You go, you get.

POPPY: Just … family shit, you know?

SKY: Families suck.

POPPY: The worst.

SKY: Ohmygod, I've just had the best idea. You should do the Grammar test too. You'll totally smash it. Then we can still be together.

POPPY: What? But you don't even want to go.

SKY*'s phone rings.*

SKY: Alright! I'm coming! Nagging bitch!

SCENE THREE

Poppy's house.

POPPY: Stop.

HEATHER: Oh, come on. Do you want to be the only one at this party who doesn't have something decent to wear?

POPPY: Don't be ridiculous. It's Sasha's house.

HEATHER: But they're all getting new stuff, aren't they? The shoes and everything. I've seen the photos.

POPPY: How?

HEATHER: I do actually follow you, remember? Just 'cause I don't comment.

POPPY: Thank god for that.

HEATHER: You're welcome.

POPPY: Anyway, I know you don't have the money so you can stop pretending it's just hidden away somewhere.

HEATHER: I can take some out of the emergency pot.

POPPY: A dress is not an emergency.

HEATHER: How much do you have right now?

POPPY: Five bucks. Total.

HEATHER: I get paid Friday week. When's the party?

POPPY: This Saturday.

HEATHER: —

POPPY: Why don't you ever go back and chase the child support money?

HEATHER: There's no point, is there?

POPPY: He has to pay you. It's the law.

HEATHER: I can do this on my own.

POPPY: So it's just me nobody cares about?

HEATHER: I care about you. Obviously. I love you.

POPPY: —

HEATHER: Next time. Okay?

POPPY: Sky's going to Grammar.

HEATHER: Oh?

POPPY: It's all her dad's idea.

HEATHER: Is it?

POPPY: He's going on about how it's normal to want the best for your kids. Get some good grades. Get into uni.

HEATHER: Yeah.

POPPY: They got her a tutor so she can pass the entrance exam.

HEATHER: Do you think she'll pass?

POPPY: Even if she doesn't they'll find a way to get her in. That's what they're like.

HEATHER: Good for her.

POPPY: She'll go way better than me at a school like that. Get a great job. Get a great life.

HEATHER: You'll get a great job. You'll have a great life.

POPPY: I'll never see her again anyway so I guess it doesn't make any difference.

HEATHER: Don't be silly. She's your friend.

POPPY: You don't understand.

HEATHER: I understand more than you think.

POPPY: Just forget it.

HEATHER: No, come on—

POPPY: It's fine! Forget it!

Pause.

HEATHER: Am I ruining your life now? Is that it? Am I the worst mother ever?

POPPY: God. I wish I'd never said anything.

SCENE FOUR

School playing field. POPPY *and* SKY. SKY *is busy on her phone.*

SKY: Why is your mum such a tight-arse anyway?
POPPY: Sucks, right? Maybe I should get like a job or something.

> POPPY *blinks in a prounced way—the blinking tic.*

SKY: Ugh. Boredom.
POPPY: I saw the perfect dress yesterday.
SKY: Yeah?
POPPY: Shop window, front and centre.
SKY: Damn.
POPPY: It's like, white. Or maybe cream. With a slash across here. And very … you know?
SKY: We have a party to go to. You need to get that dress before someone else does.
POPPY: Yeah I do.

> POPPY *does the blinking tic.*

SKY: Any normal mother would just give you the money.
POPPY: I know. She's full-on bank account bitch.

> POPPY *does the blinking tic.*

Pass me your phone.
SKY: Ohmygod, did you see Lily's shoes?

> SKY *hands her phone over.* POPPY *taps in.* SKY *looks at* POPPY *for the first time in this conversation.*

POPPY: —

> POPPY *does the blinking tic.*

SKY: They're like Gaga goes to law school. Go to Insta.
POPPY: Wait, I'm looking up the dress.

> POPPY *does the blinking tic.*

See, look, look. Oh my god.
SKY: What is that?
POPPY: Check the price. That's insane.

> POPPY *does the blinking tic.*

SKY: No, that thing you're doing with your eyes.
POPPY: What thing?
SKY: Stop blinking at me.
POPPY: I'm I'm I'm I'm I'm—
SKY: What? Stop weirding me out.
POPPY: God, sorry. What the hell? It's really bright out here, hey?
SKY: So what are you gonna do?
POPPY: Huh?
SKY: About the dress?
POPPY: I have to get it.
SKY: Just take her credit card.
POPPY: —

> POPPY *does the blinking tic.*

SKY: Bet she won't even notice …
POPPY: —

> POPPY *does the blinking tic.*

SKY: Poppy.
POPPY: Yeah?
SKY: You're doing it.
POPPY: Yeah, I am. I'm going to go for it.
SKY: No, your eyes. You're doing the eye thing.
POPPY: I'm—

> POPPY *does the blinking tic.*

I'm going to get what I want.
SKY: Stop doing that. You're making me want to blink.
POPPY: It's really bright out here.
SKY: So buy some sunglasses!

SCENE FIVE

POPPY *is in the dress shop.* SHOP GIRL *is on her phone.* SKY *is outside, but on the phone to* POPPY.

SHOP GIRL: Yeah, no, it's because of the patriarchy. Or capitalism. I
    forget which.
POPPY: You go, you get.

SKY: Go on.

POPPY: I'm going in.

SKY: So mine is like a grey sort of cream more than a white sort of cream—

POPPY: Door alarm bleeps at me.

SKY: So make sure it's not the same.

POPPY: But shop girl waves me through.

SHOP GIRL: Like when you're really screwed up about something and nobody seems to notice so you wish someone would just run you over so everything could just stop for a minute?

POPPY: Shop's like an oven inside.

SHOP GIRL: Am I right?

SKY: I love new things.

POPPY: Light bouncing off the mirrors—

SKY: They make everything …

POPPY: Rushing into my eyes-nose-ears-head—

SKY: Just …

POPPY: Pounding.

SKY: Better.

POPPY: Stop.

SHOP GIRL: Seriously, just take it out for a walk, you know? Give it some air.

POPPY: Close my eyes.

Just nervous is all, don't over think …

Now … open.

See?

[blink, blink, blink]

SKY: Okay, do you see it?

POPPY: All normal.

SKY: Is it still in the window?

POPPY: Run my hand along the sleeves.

Cotton, cotton, silk, wool,

cashmere probably.

SHOP GIRL: That is exactly what I said to her, babe. A hundred per cent.

POPPY: Everything one hundred per cent …

No cheap blends in here.

SKY: This could actually be a really big deal …
POPPY: All perfectly positioned to make you feel special.
SKY: It might not be as lame as you think—
POPPY: Quality.
SKY: And who wants to take the risk?
POPPY: New smells …

> *She breathes in deeply.*

Mmm …
[blink]
SHOP GIRL: I know … I'm like an expert on this stuff now.
POPPY: I need this.
I deserve this.
[blink blink]
SKY: [*to someone off*] Coming!
SHOP GIRL: Slow day in here you can practically do a whole PhD on
your phone.
POPPY: Hand along the hanging sleeves.
SKY: [*to someone off*] Alright!
POPPY: Shop girl's on her screen with her boyfriend, girlfriend.
SHOP GIRL: But I mean what the hell would I know?
SKY: Nagging bitch.
POPPY: Cotton, cotton, silk …
SHOP GIRL: I'm just a shop girl.
SKY: Damn it. Poppy …
POPPY: Yes.
SKY: I have to go.
POPPY: This is the dress.
This one.

> SKY *hangs up.*

SHOP GIRL: God, maybe I should go back to uni and study
psychology or something.
POPPY: Quick slide under bleached wood hanger.
One flick and
shoulders tumble silently into my palm.
Then one-eighty rotation to face the shop girl,

line it up over the bag behind me
and it's in.
My dress.

    POPPY *faints.* SHOP GIRL *rushes over.*

SHOP GIRL: Ohmygodohmygod! Hello? Can you hear me? This is
exactly what I need. [*On the phone*] I'll call you back. [*To* POPPY]
Hello? Miss? What do I … what do I … can you hear me?

    POPPY *wakes up.*

Ohthankgod, I thought you were like dead or something.
POPPY: What?
SHOP GIRL: You just totally fell over all over the place.
POPPY: Oh, my head.
SHOP GIRL: Are you okay?
POPPY: —
    [blink, blink, blink, blink, blink]
SHOP GIRL: Is everything—?
POPPY: Where's my bag?
SHOP GIRL: Right here. Do you want me to get something out for
you?
POPPY: No, it's fine.
SHOP GIRL: Do you want to like sit down or whatever?
POPPY: No. No no no.
SHOP GIRL: I keep telling them to fix the air con.
POPPY: It's nothing. Everything's fine. Isn't it?
SHOP GIRL: Uh … I guess.
POPPY: See? No problem.
SHOP GIRL: Okay. If you say so. Otherwise I have to fill out a form
and …
POPPY: No! No form.
Everything's fine.
SHOP GIRL: You sure?
POPPY: Just leave me alone!
SHOP GIRL: Jeez. Okay. Well … enjoy your shopping I guess.

SCENE SIX

Sasha's house.

SASHA: So I reckon we're up to like eighty for the party, maybe a hundred if the church kids come. I told my mum fifty, but yeah, she'll be cool either way. I'll just get Dad to run out for extra supplies if there's heaps of people.

POPPY: Wait, are they going to be here?

SASHA: Huh?

POPPY: Your parents.

SASHA: No way. Don't tell your mum.

POPPY: So how are they going to run out for beers?

SASHA: I'll text them what we need.

POPPY: They won't mind?

SASHA: Are you kidding? They'll be happy for me having so many friends.

POPPY: I guess the church kids won't wreck the joint.

SASHA: You wait. This party's going to be epic. Hey. You want to have a smoke?

POPPY: A cigarette?

SASHA: Nah … you know …

POPPY: Your mum's downstairs.

SASHA: We'll just open the window. Come on.

POPPY: Yeah, no.

SASHA: Don't you do it?

POPPY: I mean I don't really feel like it right now.

SASHA: Yeah, sure. We can have it later.

POPPY: Sure.

Hey, I got a new dress for the party. Just now. What do you think?

She pulls the dress out of her bag.

I chucked the bag. Hate plastic, don't you?

SASHA: Uh, I guess. Yeah.

POPPY *holds the dress up against her to see how it looks. It's way too grown-up for her.*

POPPY: So what do you think?

SASHA: Wow. It's very … sophisticated.

POPPY: Right?

SASHA: Where'd you get it?

POPPY: From that … that …

> POPPY *does the blinking tic.*

Shit!

> *And again.*

That shop in the city, the—

> POPPY *tries to shake it off but the blink won't stop. It turns into a spasm.*

that shop we all …

SASHA: In the city? Go you with the cash splash! Put it on, let's see.

> *The spasm is taking over* POPPY*'s body. Her neck, her arm.*

What are you doing?

POPPY: I don't know, I—

> *The spasm continues.*

Whoa. God! Come on!

> POPPY *tries to put on the dress. The spasm continues …*

SASHA: Stop mucking around, Poppy.

> POPPY *struggles to control herself, in a kind of dance of death with the dress.*

POPPY: I can't stop! I can't—

> *The spasm gets worse.*

SASHA: Okay, now you're scaring me.

POPPY: Shit! Come on!

> POPPY *manages to get the dress on but the spasm doesn't stop and she is shaking out of control. This spasm will become one of her tics.* SASHA *tries to restrain her.*

Let me go!

SASHA: Mum!

POPPY: No, don't!

> SASHA *lets go and* POPPY *pulls the dress off. But her movements go mad.*

SASHA: Mum! Where are you?

POPPY: —

    [tic tic tic]

SASHA: We need some help up here. Mum!?

POPPY: —

    [spasm, spasm, tic]

    Mum?

SASHA: She's coming.

POPPY: I want my—

    [tic, tic, tic, tic]

    I—I—I—I—

        She looks like she's having an epileptic fit. SASHA *starts filming*
        POPPY *on her phone.* LUCY *enters.*

LUCY: Sasha? What's going … Oh my lord!

POPPY: I—I—I—I—

SASHA: Oh my god!

LUCY: Sasha! Stop that!

SCENE SEVEN

POPPY *films herself on her phone.*

POPPY: Hi.

    [tic, tic]

    My name's Poppy.

    This is my first time on YouTube.

    Hi.

    [tic, tic]

    I've got this thing you can see

    [tic, tic, tic]

    that's happening to my body.

    It's pretty weird. It just sort of

    [tic]

    started.

    [tic]

    See that? I can't control it. And I don't know what it is.

    So I was wondering

    [tic, tic]

has anyone else ever had this?
And … like …
[tic, tic, tic, tic, tic]
What's going to happen to me?

    She uploads.

SCENE EIGHT

Poppy's house. Breakfast. POPPY *holds a box of cereal.*

HEATHER: So tired this morning. Had to stay back late last night.
Love how they call it a 'restructure'. Wage slavery more like. You
sleep alright?
POPPY: Yeah. Tired.
    [tic]
HEATHER: Wouldn't be so bad if there was more notice, you know,
could have had a nap before I went in. Recharge the battery.

    POPPY *opens the cereal. She has a tic and spills some.*

HEATHER: Oops.
POPPY: Sorry.
    [tic]
HEATHER: Anyway, I'm sorry but it looks like it might be another late
one tonight—

    POPPY *eats the cereal out of the box, trying to stop her tic.*

Don't you want a bowl for that?

    POPPY *can't control the tics and the cereal goes everywhere.*

What are you doing?
Hey, hey, stop! What are you doing?

SCENE NINE

POPPY *under bright lights, being examined by* DOCTORS.

DOCTOR: Hold please. If you can.

    Flash! The DOCTORS *parade in front of her, check her heart,
eyes, ears, arms, take her temperature, do a skin prick test, put
her in an oxygen mask, take a blood sample, get her to run on
the spot, spit in a specimen jar, et cetera.*

All the while, POPPY *is beset by tics.*

HEATHER: Eye scan
 brain scan
 electro cardiogram
 speech test
 reflexes
 nothing, nothing, all—
 Did you hit your head when you fainted?
 Something you ate?
 Are you on drugs?
 What about the rest of us,
 the family?
 Any history of epilepsy?
 ADHD
 autism spectrum
 OCD
 allergies
 migraines.
 I can't think of anything.
 Anything at all?
 No. No. No. And no.
 Everything has been completely
 and utterly
 normal.
 But look at you.
 Just look.
POPPY: —
 [tic, tic, tic]
HEATHER: And then we're out of Emergency.
 Back on our own.
 And what am I supposed do?

SCENE TEN

Home.

HEATHER: You have to go back to school.
POPPY: What?

HEATHER: I'm sorry … I hate doing this.
POPPY: I can't. Not until the doctors—
HEATHER: And I have to go back to work.
POPPY: I'm not ready …
  [tic, tic]
  I look like a weirdo.
  [tic, tic, blink, blink, blink]
HEATHER: You don't look—
POPPY: Everyone at school is going to kill themselves—
HEATHER: Come on, love.
POPPY: Mum … please …
HEATHER: You know I can't afford to keep calling in sick.
POPPY: Don't then. Just go.
HEATHER: And I can't leave you here on your own. What if
  something happens?
POPPY: It won't.
HEATHER: Poppy …
POPPY: No, seriously. You should go.
HEATHER: You'll be much safer at school.
POPPY: Safer?! Do you have any idea what kids are like?
HEATHER: I've already spoken to Ms Holt and—
POPPY: Oh god, that's even worse—
  [tic, tic, tic, tic, tic]
HEATHER: Everything's going to be fine … I promise … We'll make
  this go away.
POPPY: How? By making me go away?
HEATHER: Don't be silly.
POPPY: This is so unfair.
HEATHER: I'm sorry.
POPPY: What kind of mother forces her sick child to go to school?
HEATHER: It doesn't mean I'm not worried about you. And you've
  got your phone—
POPPY: This old piece of shit—
HEATHER: that still makes phone calls. You can phone me—at
  lunch—or anytime you want.
POPPY: I have to turn it off during lessons, Heather.
HEATHER: Heather?

Pause.

Why are you calling me that?
POPPY: It's your name, isn't it?
HEATHER: I'm your mother.
POPPY: Start acting like one then.
HEATHER: Poppy!

SCENE ELEVEN

School playing field. POPPY *has a physical tic going on, not too extreme.*

POPPY: Brain test, eye test, heart test, blah blah …
SKY: —
POPPY: So, yeah, they don't really know what it is yet but …
SKY: —
POPPY: It's been worse than this.
SKY: —
POPPY: Want to go to the shops after school?
SKY: Tutor.
POPPY: So maybe tomorrow?
SKY: —
POPPY: Or we could just hang at yours. Or mine. Mum'll be working.
SKY: —
POPPY: Sky.
SKY: Hmm.
POPPY: You're staring at me.
SKY: What?
POPPY: Stop staring at me.
SKY: It's just …
POPPY: Say it.
SKY: It looks weird.
POPPY: Thanks.
SKY: You told me to say it.
POPPY: I know but—
SKY: I thought Sasha's clip was a joke but it's actually really weird now I'm looking at you.
POPPY: Did you see my YouTube?

SKY: Everyone's seen it.

POPPY: It's had loads of hits.

SKY: Some people are saying stuff …

POPPY: What stuff?

SKY: Nothing. No.

POPPY: What?!

SKY: They're just dicks anyway.

POPPY: —

SKY: Does it hurt? When you do the … things?

POPPY: Tics.

SKY: Right.

POPPY: They've got me on some meds.

SKY: But aren't you worried about … like …

POPPY: What?

SKY: I don't know like, what if I get it?

POPPY: Don't say that.

SKY: I don't want to catch it.

POPPY: Why would you catch it?

SKY: I dunno. I might.

POPPY: And anyway, I'm taking these drugs now, so it'll go really quickly.

SKY: Well, what about Sasha?

POPPY: How was the party anyway? I bet it was lame as. Is that why you didn't post anything?

SKY: You don't know?

POPPY: What?

SKY: Oh my god.

POPPY: What?! I've been practically living at the doctors, what am I supposed to know?

SKY: She's got it.

POPPY: Got what?

SKY: Same as you.

POPPY: What are you talking about?

SKY: She never even had the party 'cause she was having some kind of fit.

POPPY: I'm not having a fit.

SKY: Whatever, she was spazzing all over the place and—

POPPY: Far out.

SKY: I know. Killed my Saturday night.

POPPY: I don't understand. How can Sasha have the same thing?

SKY: I know, weird right?

POPPY: And she's got like … the twitching? All of it?

SKY: Reckon she caught it off you?

POPPY: What? No!

SKY: You had that spaz at her place.

POPPY: Yeah, but—

SKY: Shit. I know I'm going to get it next. I don't want to get it, Poppy.

Can you just stand over there a bit?

POPPY: Jesus, Sky!

MS HOLT *enters.*

MS HOLT: Here you are!

SKY: [*under her breath*] What's she doing here?

MS HOLT: I've been looking for you.

POPPY: Sorry, Miss Holt.

MS HOLT: What for?

POPPY: I don't know. Have I done something?

MS HOLT: I came to see how you're going.

POPPY: Uh … okay, I guess.

MS HOLT: It's good to see you back at school.

POPPY: Sure.

MS HOLT: Your mum asked me to check in on you.

POPPY: Her version of parenting …

MS HOLT: You girls like this spot here.

SKY: Been here since grade seven.

MS HOLT: Yes, it's not bad, is it? Got a clear view of the pitch. Good for when the boys play sport, I suppose?

SKY: [*under her breath*] Awkward.

POPPY: Um, well thanks for checking in …

MS HOLT: Another girl has just reported in sick. 'Too embarrassed' to come to school, her mother says. I'm wondering if you know her—Ashley.

POPPY: Ashley?

SKY: Shit!

MS HOLT: Sky!

SKY: Oh. Sorry.

MS HOLT: So you do know her?

POPPY: We're friends. I mean not best, but we're fine, y'know. She hangs here with us sometimes.

MS HOLT: Do you have anything else? Something you do together?

POPPY: No.

MS HOLT: A place you go outside of school?

POPPY: No.

MS HOLT: Think a bit harder.

POPPY: I can't … I can't think of anything.

MS HOLT: Nothing you're hiding from me?

SKY: Oh my god. You, Sasha and now Ashley. What the hell?

MS HOLT: We don't want things to get out of hand.

POPPY: How do you mean?

MS HOLT: We can talk it through in my office. Why don't you come and see me during first period this afternoon?

POPPY: Oh, but that's science.

MS HOLT: We've had great reports for the last couple of years. Full marks for student welfare.

SKY: Legit?

MS HOLT: I've worked very hard to get us to this point.

SKY: [*under her breath*] And the point is …?

MS HOLT: And I'm sure your friends will be happy to collect work for you if you want to go home after we talk, won't you, Sky?

SKY: Oh … uh …

MS HOLT: You're one of our brightest, Poppy—we need you back on top form.

POPPY: I'm trying.

MS HOLT: So try and think of something.

POPPY: Yes, Miss.

MS HOLT: And I'll see you later?

POPPY: Yes, Miss. Thank you, Miss.

MS HOLT *leaves.*

SKY: Ha. Sucked in or what?

POPPY: What?

SKY: She's scared of you.

POPPY: Me? No way.

SKY: Yes way. You just got like an instant extra twenty per cent.

POPPY: What, you want to swap?

SKY: Yes, Miss. Thank you, Miss.

POPPY: Be worse at Grammar. Have to curtsey there.

SKY: Shut up.

POPPY: No, you shut up. Just shut up shut up shut up!

SCENE TWELVE

POPPY: Walking home feels like peeling layers off my skin.
     The sun is too bright
     the cars are … cars are …
     [tic, tic]
     Waiting at the lights,
     a kid stares out the window of mummy's silver Jeep,
     high in his baby seat for a perfect view of me
     as my head hits the pole
     again
     and again
     and then he's crying out
     Mum-Mum-Mum!
     Nuh nuh nuh—
     Green man releases me and I walk
     raw and bleeding
     as—nuh nuh nuh—normal as I can.
     Don't step on the cracks.
     Bookshop
     clothes shop
     bakery
     homewares.
     Why are there so many—nuh nuh nuh—windows?
     [tic, tic, tic]
     I swear, when this is over,
     I will never stare at anyone ever.

SCENE THIRTEEN

Sheila's office. POPPY *has a few low-level tics. She is trying her best to hold them in.*

SHEILA: This is a fascinating case. Just … so much … I mean I'm sure we can help each other here. I'm sure I can help you.
POPPY: Right.
SHEILA: Right. So you're presenting with a range of irregular behaviours including phonic and motor tics similar to those associated with the condition Tourette's syndrome.
POPPY: Is that what this is?
SHEILA: The onset was three weeks ago?
POPPY: Three yesterday. Is that what this is?
SHEILA: And you've seen a few doctors. Still seeing your GP?
POPPY: Duh. She's the one who sent me here.
SHEILA: Yes. Are your parents outside? I should have a word with them after.
POPPY: Don't they give you, like, electric shock treatment for Tourette's?
SHEILA: Let's not get ahead of ourselves … Where are your parents?
POPPY: Mum had to go to work.
SHEILA: And your father?
POPPY: It's just me and Mum.
SHEILA: So no-one came with you today?
POPPY: No. So whatever you need to know you have to ask me, okay? And then I could ask you, like, what the hell am I doing in a psych's office and how is that going to help me?
SHEILA: I asked to see you.
POPPY: Why?
SHEILA: We have an arrangement. Me and the GP. She tells me about any interesting cases she has and I do the first sessions pro bono.
POPPY: Pro what?
SHEILA: Free.
POPPY: But why?
SHEILA: You've got to have something juicy to keep you alive in a desert like this.

POPPY: Juicy. Great.

SHEILA: And your case is … unusual … challenging.

POPPY: Fantastic.

SHEILA: How are you finding the meds?

POPPY: They make me tired.

SHEILA: I can take over as your prescribing doctor, adjust the dose. The tics don't seem too bad.

POPPY: So I'm like some kind of experiment for you.

SHEILA: Can you stop them … when you want to?

POPPY: Am I?

SHEILA: What about at school? Can you stop them there?

POPPY: Sort of. Then it's worse.

SHEILA: Have you talked to any other girls at school about what's happening to you?

POPPY: Not really.

SHEILA: Haven't confided in anyone? Not even a best friend?

POPPY: No, okay?

SHEILA: Who do you hang around with?

POPPY: What's that got to do with anything?

   Pause.

SHEILA: Tell me about home. How is everything there?

POPPY: Dunno.

SHEILA: Normal? Stressful?

POPPY: Weird.

SHEILA: Weird how?

POPPY: Yesterday I put the milk in the pantry and my shoes in the fridge. Juicy enough for you?

SHEILA: Oh, I do that sort of thing all the time.

POPPY: Bet you don't. Bet you've never done a single thing like that in your whole life. You're just saying it to make me feel better.

SHEILA: Doesn't seem to have worked.

POPPY: Wasn't even funny.

SHEILA: I have to ask you, have you had any thoughts of harming yourself?

POPPY: My body's already doing it. Look.

SHEILA: I mean by choice. Worse than that.

POPPY: …
　　Yeah.

SHEILA: What made you decide not to?

POPPY: Who says I've decided?

SHEILA: Those thoughts are not you, Poppy.You don't have to listen
　　to them.

POPPY: I'm supposed to be the smart one. I was going to be a
　　scientist.

SHEILA: What do you mean was?

POPPY: I can't even pour a bowl of cereal without getting it all over
　　myself. How am I supposed to do experiments and stuff?

SHEILA: It's all about the brain, isn't it? Creative thinking. Not
　　pouring things into bowls.

POPPY: Oh what, so I'm stuck with this?

SHEILA: No, I'm not saying that. We're going to find a solution. But
　　isn't it what's inside that counts?

POPPY: Not around here it's not.

SHEILA: Tell me what you mean.

POPPY: I mean look at me! I look like an idiot. How am I supposed to
　　dress nice, look nice? Who is ever going to want this?

SHEILA: You think people are judging you.

POPPY: Duh.

SHEILA: And that bothers you.

POPPY: Nobody wants to hang around with a retard.

SHEILA: That's not very nice language to use.

POPPY: Who cares?

SHEILA: I do.

POPPY: Maybe I should just clone myself without the broken bits.

SHEILA: Ha! Let me know how you go.

POPPY: Maybe the other me will still be popular.

SHEILA: Maybe the real you still is. Talk to your friends. Okay?

SCENE FOURTEEN

All the performers become all the infected girls.

— Like an itch, I guess
— More like an ache

— An achy sort of itch
— An achy itchy sort of tingling scratch
— No-one can even see but you can't ignore it
— It's right there
— I hear it
— A quiet howl
— Well, it's not so much a scratch as a … what?
— A snap. More like a snap
— Yeah
— Snap snap snap
— That's it. Snap snap snap like that
— And then
— Instant relief
— Yeah, really calm, you know
— The ocean
— For a second
— Just floating
— Two or three seconds maybe four
— Then
— Tingle
— Try to ignore it
— 'Cause you know it's not quite right
— But then snap snap snap snap
— Snap snap snap snap snap snap snap
— Dropped your pen
— Get out of my way
— Freak
— Books all over
— Again with the snap
— All over the floor
— Across the hall
— They can hear me
— Barking
— Yelping
— Like a zoo in here
— Eyes all over me
— All over my ugly
— And I can't stop

— This howl coming at me
— Can't stop and I'm
— I'm feeling like a freak
— Don't
— Don't say
— What?
— You can't
— Can't say freak?
— It's not right, is it?
— No
— No, 'cause we're supposed to feel sorry for people like that
— But yeah
— Because I am a freak. I'm a
— Spaz
— A nuff nuff
— Retard
— A nuftard
— A spazzo retard nuff nuff
— Yeah?
— And I don't want to be one of them
— I want to be
— What?
— Regular. Just—
— You know
— But I'm not
— And it doesn't make any difference what I want
— That's right
— 'Cause it's moved to my face
— My arm
— My lips
— Leg
— Throat
— Neck
— So much neck
— Arm slash neck slash arm slash throat slash
— Hurts a bloody lot actually
— Won't stop, won't rest

— It's like this
— I don't know a
— Roar of energy coming at me
— Howling at me
— At my arm neck throat slash whatever
— Except it's coming from inside
— Nowhere to go
— My whole body's screaming its head off
— And there's nowhere
— Where can I go?
— Just nowhere to escape this
— Screeching blinding almighty—

SCENE FIFTEEN

SASHA *alone in her room, trying to do up her buttons, twitching.*

POPPY *enters.*

POPPY: Sasha? Hey, how you going? Your mum said I could come up.
SASHA: —
    [tic, tic, tic, tic]
POPPY: Pretty bad, huh?
SASHA: Hurts. You?
POPPY: All the time. Nuh nuh nuh, feel sick, feel shit, feel—
    [tic, tic]
SASHA: What are you taking?
POPPY: Some stuff that's supposed to stop the tics.
SASHA: I'm on antibiotics. My doctor says it's
    [tic, tic]
    this autoimmune thing. You get it after you've had strep throat.
    Sometimes you don't even know you've had an infection and
    that's how it turns into this.
POPPY: So I might have had it too?
SASHA: You should get onto my doctor. He has a really long wait list
    but Mum's friends with his wife so she'll get you in easy.
POPPY: Are they working? The antibiotics?
SASHA: —
    [tic, tic, tic, tic]

I keep doing this thing where it's like I'm punching myself in the head.

POPPY: Good times.

SASHA: I have to not hold anything sharp in that hand.

POPPY: Death by tic stabbing! Far out!

SASHA: Yeah, way to go.

POPPY: They sent me to a shrink.

SASHA: Some chick on the north side?

POPPY: Did you go there too? What did she tell you?

SASHA: Nothing. Mum went in for like two minutes then marched out saying, 'We're leaving'.

POPPY: Why?

SASHA: Says it's not my brain that's the problem.

POPPY: Do you know if Ashley went to the same place?

SASHA: It's not just Ashley now. There's Bronte, some girls in the next grade, and you know that super blond girl, what's her name, Olivia?

POPPY: Jesus. How do you know all this?

SASHA: Mum told me.

POPPY: Who told her?

SASHA: She just knows stuff. That's why she cancelled the party, 'cause she found out we're not the only ones who've got it. I've still got your dress. You want it?

POPPY: I guess.

SASHA *pulls it out from somewhere. Very rumpled.*

SASHA: You would have looked really hot.

POPPY: I would have been so good.

SASHA: The whole thing …

POPPY: Screw it. Let's have the party anyway.

SASHA: What?

POPPY: Right now. Let's have the party now. Put some music on. I'm not going to let this thing stop us.

SASHA: This thing. We don't even have a name for it.

POPPY: Let's give it one then. How about The Chaos?

They're dancing now, with the dress as a partner, with their tics as partners.

SASHA: The Touch.

POPPY: Ticplosion.

SASHA: Smackface.

POPPY: Spazilla.

SASHA: Freakhead.

POPPY: Fred.

SASHA: What?

POPPY: I'm calling this tic Fred. Because it's not me doing this stupid thing. It's stupid old Fred. And this one here is Janet. She's an idiot. And this is … Tallulah!

Hey, let's introduce everyone to the world.

She uses her phone to film them dancing.

Hello, world! Here we are!

SASHA: You're mad!

POPPY: I'm mad! Look at me! Hell yeah! Crazy mad like the church kids!

SASHA: Hey.

We should stop.

POPPY: What?

SASHA: Stop it. Turn it off. Turn it off!

POPPY: What's wrong?

SASHA: That's the old me. I need to be better now.

POPPY: What are you talking about?

SASHA: Maybe this is all my fault. Maybe I deserve this. Do you think god's punishing me?

POPPY: What for?

SASHA: I got the throat infection after I made out with James Richardson.

POPPY: So?

SASHA: It's a sin.

POPPY: Kissing?

SASHA: I let him finger me too.

POPPY: I thought it was supposed to be okay as long as you didn't do it properly, like with your real parts.

SASHA: Nah. It's all bad. Mum's got her prayer group doing overtime.

POPPY: You told her?!

SASHA: No way. But god knows. And sometimes I think she's got him on speed dial, so she probably knows too.

POPPY: Shit.

SASHA: I'm going to say a prayer. Ask forgiveness for the dancing. And … the James stuff.

SASHA *kneels.* POPPY *waits.*

Come on.

POPPY: I'm not really into praying.

SASHA: Please. We have to.

POPPY: But I don't believe in—

SASHA: I don't want this thing, Poppy, I hate it, I hate it for both of us. It's like an alien inside me, I feel so ugly, so pointless and diseased and—

POPPY: Okay, okay.

They kneel.

If god's punishing you, does that mean he's punishing me too? And what about Ashley? I mean, if you made out with James—

LUCY *enters.*

LUCY: I'm sorry to be interrupting.

POPPY: Oh hi, Mrs Porter!

LUCY: Oh, I'm so happy to see you girls praying. I know we can solve this together with god's love and the love we show each other.

I'll come back when you've finished.

POPPY: No, it's good. We were nearly done and I have to go anyway.

LUCY: But you have to finish your prayers. You can't stop halfway.

Why don't I join you?

SASHA: There's space here, Mum.

LUCY: Thank you, darling.

Go ahead, Poppy. You lead.

POPPY: I'm not really a regular …

LUCY: Don't worry about that.

POPPY: I don't know what I'm supposed to say.

LUCY: Say anything at all. He'll hear you.

POPPY: Okay. Um … nuh nuh nuh …

Dear god.

Hello.

I'm Poppy … I guess you know that—nuh nuh nuh—shit! Sorry.

LUCY: Go on.

POPPY: Um … I don't know if you can hear me but Sasha says you
can fix this thing we've got—

[tic, tic, tic]

Oh, ha ha! That's funny, not—nuh nuh nuh—

[tic, tic, tic, tic, tic, tic]

Shit. Where are you?! Are you here?

> *She hits herself in the head.*

LUCY: Poppy—

POPPY: Or are you in here? Make it go away.

You can do that, right? Come on, show us a miracle! Or maybe
you can't because it's all bullshit!

LUCY: Poppy!

POPPY: —

[tic, tic, tic, tic, tic]

Yeah, well screw you!

LUCY: Shut your mouth!

SASHA: Mum …

LUCY: You can go now.

POPPY: Sorry.

LUCY: Just go.

POPPY: Fine. 'Bye, Sash. See you at school.

LUCY: Oh no, Sasha will be staying home until she's better. School
can wait.

SCENE SIXTEEN

Poppy's house.

POPPY: —

[tic, tic]

You said you'd help fix this.

HEATHER: I want to, love, I really do. But, Lucy and the other mums,
I'm not sure that's the right way to go.

POPPY: It's just a coffee. Ask them how all the girls are. What are
they taking? What does your doctor say? What does hers say?

[tic]

They're all going to different doctors and they're all totally
cashed-up so it'll be top people, specialists, no stone unturned,
I mean eight different med-heads trying to work it out, one of
them's got to know what's going on and all you have to do is ask
them.

HEATHER: They'd probably make up some excuse and say no.

    Pause.

POPPY: They don't know you're working at Coles.

HEATHER: Where do they think I work?

POPPY: At a law firm.

HEATHER: And the night shifts?

POPPY: International clients.

HEATHER: Pop …

POPPY: Well, it's only temporary, isn't it?

HEATHER: What about Sky?

POPPY: Haven't seen her.

HEATHER: You two are like glue.

POPPY: Guess she doesn't like freaks now.

HEATHER: I'm sorry, love.

POPPY: Not sorry enough to have a coffee.

HEATHER: Sweetheart …

POPPY: I hate you.

HEATHER: Oh, Pops.

POPPY: I do.

HEATHER: Don't say that.

POPPY: —

    [tic]
    It's just a cup of coffee.
    [tic, tic]
    Don't you want me to get better?

SCENE SEVENTEEN

Poppy's room. POPPY *tries to brush her hair—a new tic appears, hair
is a mess.*

POPPY: Goddam it.

She checks herself in her phone.

Not as if anyone's looking at my hair.

HEATHER *calls from downstairs.*

HEATHER: Dinner!
POPPY: Not hungry!
HEATHER: It's your favourite! Spaghetti bol!
POPPY: Cancer.
HEATHER: I'll cut it up for you!
POPPY: I said I'm not hungry! Leave me alone!

Back to her phone.

MSG TO SKY: Hey. Wanna get coffee? Doctor's orders.

Nothing.

MSG TO SKY: Need to download. U there?

Nothing.

MSG TO SKY: Hello????!!!! ☺ ☺ ☺

POPPY *takes a selfie. Sends it to* SKY.

MSG TO SKY: Hahahaha looking like a total spaz right now

Nothing.

MSG TO SKY: U ignoring me??????

Nothing.

POPPY: Okay then, I'll go public.
Status: Stuffed in the head. Bring caffeine stat!

She tags Sky.

The following social media comments in very quick succession:

— U look like shit
— Don't think coffee's gunna help you
— Hahahahaha
— Spaz hed
— What RU doing on here?
— Go back to the zoo where you belong
— Retard freak
— Infected

— Yeah get off my feed don't want yr germs
— Toxic dog
— Woof woof
— Dog face spaz
— Don't u know everyone hates you
— I bet your parents dream about putting a pillow over your head at
    night
SKY: WTF? How did I get on this thread?
— U friends with dog spaz?
— Gunna get spazzed
— Seriously if that happened to me id do a full suicide
SKY: *Untag me!*

SCENE EIGHTEEN

Ms Holt's office.

MS HOLT: Where's Sky? I told her to come too.
POPPY: We're not talking so I don't—
MS HOLT: And why didn't you come and see me the other day? We
    were going to have that chat?
POPPY: Oh. Yeah … I was probably at the doctor's.
MS HOLT: You're not in trouble, you know.
POPPY: Yes, Miss.
MS HOLT: Have you been sitting in your regular spot? On the field?
POPPY: I've been away quite a bit.
MS HOLT: Probably a good thing as it turns out.
POPPY: Miss?
MS HOLT: Yes?
POPPY: I have basketball practice in second-half lunch.
MS HOLT: You're still doing basketball?
POPPY: Not that there are any games but—
MS HOLT: Yes, that's my point. You've seen that van outside?
POPPY: Giant aerial on top?
MS HOLT: It's a mobile broadcasting unit. TV cameras.
POPPY: Yeah, I got that. What are they doing here?
MS HOLT: Digging up a story.
POPPY: On me?

MS HOLT: On everyone. Apparently there's some suggestion of toxins causing the … condition … perhaps something ingested … or something you've all come into frequent contact with …

POPPY: I'm not allergic to anything. We tried all that.

MS HOLT: Okay, look, someone wrote a letter to the paper. There was a chemical spill nearby—it was a very long time ago. Part of the materials used to build up the sports grounds may have come from the area around the spill and this letter talked about neurological disorders being caused by the same sort of toxins. It's only a theory but it seems the network is running with it.

POPPY: Toxins … shit … I should have thought of that before.

MS HOLT: It's nothing to do with the school.

POPPY: So why are they here?

MS HOLT: Honestly, we've tested the soil, the air conditioning, the water supply, the pot plants, everything. And there's no evidence to support this theory. But at this stage the condition only seems to be affecting our students so … yeah … they're taking it seriously.

POPPY: You said we were safe.

MS HOLT: You are. I promise.

POPPY: So?

MS HOLT: The Department has issued a directive that no student or staff should talk to the reporters. But I've been thinking … if you happened to decide to go against that directive … what you might want to say.

POPPY: I get it. You want me to give it some publicity, get the Department to hurry up and do something.

MS HOLT: Ah, well … more like … and look, you don't have to admit anything to me directly … but I know you kids all take … substances … when you're out at parties and such like. If you told the reporters that you'd taken something outside of the school … and maybe you had some kind of bad reaction …

POPPY: Substances?

MS HOLT: Uh … yes

POPPY: What do you mean exactly?

MS HOLT: Come on, Poppy.

POPPY: Come on what?

MS HOLT: You want me to spell it out?

POPPY: Spell what out, Miss Holt? I don't actually know what you're talking about so—

MS HOLT: Drugs.

POPPY: I'm sorry?

MS HOLT: I'm talking about—

POPPY: I won't do it.

MS HOLT: You won't get in trouble. It's just to give us some air. I'm saying it might be helpful, that's all. We're looking at every possible cause and these things take time.

POPPY: I didn't take drugs.

MS HOLT: If that's what you're saying then I believe you. Absolutely. I still think if they were to infer a certain background it might be useful and—

POPPY: Useful for who?

MS HOLT: I hope you don't think this benefits me in any way? The welfare of the student body is my primary concern.

POPPY: The student body? What about my welfare?! What about my body?

SCENE NINETEEN

Silence.

POPPY: Hello?

   Nothing.

   Hello?

   Nothing.

   Hello?

SASHA: [*whispering*] Poppy?

POPPY: Sasha?

   Nothing.

   Hello?

SASHA: Look, I'm not supposed to—

POPPY: Sasha, it's just me.

SASHA: Mum says I can't be online with you.

POPPY: But why?

SASHA: If she finds out she'll take my phone away.
POPPY: Sasha!

    Nothing.

  Hello?

SCENE TWENTY

Sheila's office. New tics have arrived.

SHEILA: Just relax.
POPPY: Nuh nuh nuh—none
   [tic]
  of the
   [tic]
  other girls
   [tic, tic]
SHEILA: Take your time.
POPPY: girls are
   [tic]
  nuh nuh nuh—talking
   [tic]
  to me.
SHEILA: I'm sorry to hear that.
POPPY: Bet you are.
SHEILA: Thank you for coming back.
POPPY: Because—nuh nuh nuh—
   [tic]
  you
   [tic, tic, tic]
SHEILA: Are you still taking your medi—
POPPY: Don't cut me!
   [tic]
SHEILA: I'm sorry.
POPPY: You still want to—nuh nuh nuh—poke
   [tic]
  around—nuh nuh nuh—inside—nuh nuh nuh—inside my brain.
SHEILA: I think we have more work to do.

POPPY: No we don't.

SHEILA: You're angry.

POPPY: —

　　[tic, tic]

　　Course I'm angry—nuh nuh nuh—shit yeah.

SHEILA: You're getting very worked up. You need to calm down.

POPPY: I have—nuh nuh nuh—nuh nuh nuh—

SHEILA: You feel like you're making progress?

POPPY: The answer!

　　[tic, tic]

SHEILA: Oh. What is it?

POPPY: It's from the soil,

　　[tic, tic]

　　toxins got inside—nuh nuh nuh—my brain and did this. You have
　　to—nuh nuh nuh—tell the others.

　　I know there are others.

　　[tic, tic, tic]

　　You know there are others.

SHEILA: Patient confidentiality means I can't—

POPPY: Don't bullshit me!

SHEILA: It extends to you too.

POPPY: Tell them! We're all

　　[tic, tic]

　　the same!

SHEILA: You might be, yes.

POPPY: See! I knew it!

SHEILA: Or at least affecting each other the same. A kind of
　　understanding.

POPPY: What?

SHEILA: Poppy, have you heard of the idea that your body can
　　respond in a physical way to something going on in your mind?

POPPY: What do you mean?

SHEILA: It's called psychological conversion disorder. It means
　　that the symptoms you are experiencing feel real but that the
　　underlying cause might be psychological rather than neurological.

POPPY: What? You think it's not real?

SHEILA: I think your body believes it's real.

POPPY: How can that happen? I don't get it.

SHEILA: Maybe it makes you feel a little bit different? Having this. A little bit special?

POPPY: Oh, now this is really screwed.

SHEILA: I think we need to work out what's going on in your head.

POPPY: What about the others?

SHEILA: As I say, there may be an influence of sorts.

POPPY: What about the toxins?

SHEILA: Unproven.

POPPY: That's enough.

SHEILA: Yes?

POPPY: I don't want you to treat me anymore.

SHEILA: I understand you're very confused right now.

POPPY: I withdraw my permission for you to treat me.

  [tic, tic]

SHEILA: I'm trying to help you, Poppy, and I really feel like we're making progress.

POPPY: I withdraw my permission—

SHEILA: You can't.

POPPY: What?

SHEILA: I'm sorry, but I don't need your permission. You're a minor. Your mother signed the forms.

POPPY: Nuh nuh nuh—nuh nuh nuh—

SHEILA: So, shall we continue?

POPPY: Liar!

  [tic]

  She wasn't even here.

SHEILA: You can call me what you like, I don't mind, it's a safe space here. And that's exactly what I told your mother in our session.

POPPY: No no. My mother wouldn't come here. Nuh nuh nuh—Mum and I, we stick together.

SHEILA: Your mother thinks this is what's best for you. We all do.

POPPY: All?

SHEILA: There are others who feel the same way.

POPPY: Nuh nuh nuh—not all. Not all. Nuh nuh nuh—
  Not me.

SCENE TWENTY-ONE

HEATHER *and* POPPY, LUCY *on the phone.*

HEATHER: I called Lucy. Sasha's mum.
POPPY: I knew you would.
HEATHER: Didn't want to but I did.
POPPY: I told her you're on my side.
HEATHER: Haven't spoken for a while.
LUCY: Hello?
HEATHER: A year … more?
LUCY: Who is this?
POPPY: Okay. Then?
HEATHER: It's Heather here. Poppy's mum.
POPPY: You had coffee, right? You talked. She brought the others. You all—
LUCY: Heather?
HEATHER: Wait.
POPPY: Okay. Then?
HEATHER: I'm calling about the girls. About Sasha—
LUCY: Sasha? You have the hide to talk about—
POPPY: What?
LUCY: my daughter?
HEATHER: and Poppy—
LUCY: Poppy. Yes, I know all about her.
HEATHER: They all know.
POPPY: Of course they know.
HEATHER: Yes.
LUCY: I suppose you want to say sorry.
HEATHER: What for?
LUCY: Well, I don't want to hear it.
POPPY: So you had coffee. You talked. She brought the others. You all—
HEATHER: No, that's not—
LUCY: But since you called
HEATHER: That's not what happened.
POPPY: What happened?

LUCY: I have something to say

POPPY: Did you actually see her?

LUCY: about that wicked, spiteful girl of yours.

POPPY: You didn't see her, did you?

HEATHER: She said terrible things.

LUCY: She's brainwashing our children, poisoning their minds.

HEATHER: They flew out of her mouth like crows.

LUCY: She's got some sort of a hold on my daughter.

POPPY: What?

LUCY: On all of them

HEATHER: That it's your fault

LUCY: Is she trying to start a cult?

POPPY: That's—

LUCY: Possessing them,

HEATHER: That you're somehow

LUCY: making them think they're sick

HEATHER: involved in a kind of hoax.

LUCY: and the girls believe it. They think it's real.

POPPY: It's not true.

HEATHER: Poppy?

LUCY: Your daughter

HEATHER: My Pops?

LUCY: making my daughter sick.

POPPY: Me?

LUCY: All of them because of you.

POPPY: But why?

LUCY: Why is she always over here instead of at home with her family?

HEATHER: You tell me.

POPPY: What?

LUCY: No supervision, no control.

HEATHER: Why would she say that about you?

POPPY: You said no, didn't you?

LUCY: She was the first.

HEATHER: You were the first.

POPPY: It doesn't make sense

LUCY: It makes sense.

POPPY: You—

LUCY: You have to make her stop.

POPPY: Oh my god.

LUCY: People are avoiding us.

POPPY: You believe them.

LUCY: Cutting us out of their lives.

POPPY: Don't you?

LUCY: Your daughter's the one who needs to be cut out.

POPPY: Your own daughter.

LUCY: She's a bad influence.

HEATHER: What?

LUCY: And whose fault is that? Huh?

POPPY: Is that why you made me stay at the shrink?

LUCY: Is that why she's seeing a shrink?

HEATHER: How do you know that?

POPPY: You signed the forms to keep me there.

LUCY: I know things.

HEATHER: Oh god.

POPPY: Oh my god.

LUCY: Maybe I shouldn't have said anything.

HEATHER: I'm not a doctor. I'm doing my best.

POPPY: I can't believe this.

LUCY: I'm glad I have.

HEATHER: I'm on my own here, Poppy. I don't know what else to do.

LUCY: Now it's out there. People know.

SCENE TWENTY-TWO

POPPY: I'm a virus spreading across town.
>
> Cracks in the pavement open up when they feel me walking
> towards them
> hoping to swallow me whole.
> Neutralise me.

— Shutters shut shut

POPPY: At the gourmet, lifestyle, gluten-free, spaz-free café
> here in the window I'm
> jerking around
> like chips in a deep fat fryer …

[tic, tic, tic, tic, tic, tic]
See?
See me?
— Cross the road
— Just in case
POPPY: Across the road—
   Is that—?
   Yes, yes it is.
   There, with the coffee-queue Grammar girls
   Faces shining, laughing, laughing like—
— Sky!
POPPY: Sky, over here!
   [tic, tic]
   Sky turns red,
   turns round
— Quick quick walk.
POPPY: but I'm already like,
   Hi! Hey! How are you!?
SKY: Oh.
POPPY: You good?
SKY: Yeah … You?
POPPY: Not really, but—nuh nuh nuh …
SKY: Well … I've gotta—
POPPY: You hanging with Grammar girls already?
SKY: Just, y'know …
POPPY: No.
   [tic]
SKY: You've hardly been at school anyway …
POPPY: It's okay. I forgive you.
SKY: What?
POPPY: I forgive you. Nuh nuh nuh—You thought you could catch it
   off me. That's what everyone else—nuh nuh nuh—I don't blame
   you.
SKY: What, have you found god now?
POPPY: No. I have the answer.
   [tic]
SKY: The hell are you on about?

POPPY: Miss Holt told me. There's toxic stuff in the soil, under the playing fields, getting into our brains like an infection.

[tic]

That's what's doing this.

SKY: Why haven't I got it then?

POPPY: I dunno.

SKY: 'Cause I was hanging out on the fields a whole term before you.

POPPY: Maybe you're immune. That's why we have to get the doctors to analyse it so they know which drugs to give us. Maybe they can test your blood. You might be the vaccine.

SKY: Sure.

> SKY *turns to go.*

POPPY: Wait. Nuh nuh nuh. Where are you going?

SKY: I'm leaving, remember?

POPPY: The others aren't talking to me. Their parents have gone mad, telling them they can't see me. But you're okay. You're still fine and you were there at the beginning, so you know it's not because of me and you just have to help me and show them you're okay then they'll all have to believe me. Right?

[tic, tic]

And we can shut this thing down.

SKY: Shut up, okay?

POPPY: What?

SKY: They're looking at us.

POPPY: No they're not.

SKY: Are too.

POPPY: So?

[tic]

SKY: Just leave me alone.

POPPY: What? Sky, you're supposed to be my friend.

> SKY *shrugs.*

You haven't even passed the exam yet. What if they don't want you? Nuh nuh nuh—nuh nuh nuh—What if they think you're already infected? Bet they do.

SKY: Do not.

POPPY: Look, they're walking away.

SKY: Jesus. You really know how to ruin everything. The party wasn't enough for you?

POPPY: What? That was Sasha!

SKY: Whatever.

SKY *goes to leave.*

POPPY: Sky, please! I need your help. I mean I really, really need you. I don't think I can do this on my own.

SKY: Do what?

POPPY: I spoke to the reporters.

SKY: And?

POPPY: They want me to go on TV.

SKY: So?

POPPY: They want to do a whole feature, interview my friend group and everything.

[tic]

None of the others are talking to me …

SKY: Sucks.

POPPY: I miss you.

SKY: —

POPPY: Legends …

SKY: —

POPPY: Will you do the TV thing with me? Please?

SKY: I'm not famous like you.

POPPY: This is your chance to stick it up the school.

SKY: I'm leaving anyway.

POPPY: So why not give Holt a run for her money? She's trying to stop the media finding stuff out.

SKY: Legit?

POPPY: Yeah, so she can keep her cushy job. I mean what does she even do except tell people off? Did you know enrolments are down? She's keeping that quiet too, isn't she?

SKY: Cow.

POPPY: You can say whatever you like about her—anything. I mean anything. It's easy for her to go, 'Oh yeah, these things take time'. But I don't have time. I might be dying here.

SKY: I should probably check with my dad.

POPPY: You could be next.

SKY: Don't say that.

POPPY: Until we fix this thing, it could be anybody. Why not you? Everyone's getting it.

SKY: Shit.

POPPY: I know.

SKY: I mean, I can't stand Holt.

POPPY: If this was the field at Grammar they'd be on it in a flash.

SKY: Given.

POPPY: Yeah, so we have to stand together. Normal and freak, side by side. Show the others you're not afraid.

[tic]

SKY: I'm not afraid.

POPPY: I knew I could trust you.

> POPPY *goes to hold* SKY*'s hand.* SKY *pulls away.*

SKY: Ohmygod!

POPPY: What?

SKY: TV. I have to change. You're not wearing that, are you?

SCENE TWENTY-THREE

Home. A 'For Sale' sign is up.

HEATHER: I don't have to ask you. I'm the mum. I make my own decisions.

POPPY: Come home to change my clothes and I'm like, whoa! My house is for sale? Nearly didn't recognise it behind that giant advertising board. The space! The light! The quality finishes! Footsteps to chic village lifestyle!

[tic, tic, tic]

HEATHER: It's my house … and selling it is the best thing for both of us … I should have done it ages ago.

POPPY: But where will we live?

HEATHER: We'll get a new place.

POPPY: You can't buy a house round here. You can't even buy a dress.

HEATHER: I don't want to stay here. We'll go somewhere else … somewhere far away … a healthy place, with fresh air to get you back to normal, and new people, and I won't have to work so much so we can spend more time together and—

POPPY: What, like a new school?

HEATHER: New school, new everything.

POPPY: No-one would know us.

HEATHER: Yes! A clean start … be whoever we want to be. Reinvent ourselves!

POPPY: Why?

HEATHER: I can't stay here. I'm done with this place. I can't stay around people who hate us … that woman.

POPPY: What woman?

HEATHER: All of them … Lucy … any of them.

POPPY: What about my friends?

HEATHER: They're not talking to you, Poppy. They're not your friends.

POPPY: They are!

HEATHER: I thought this would make you happy.

POPPY: —

[tic, tic]

I just wish things were like before.

[tic, tic]

Before everything got screwed up.

HEATHER: Name me one thing in this world that isn't screwed up. One thing.

POPPY: You're not supposed to say things like that. Nuh nuh nuh—nuh nuh nuh—You're the mum. Remember?

HEATHER: I do remember! It's all I ever think about. I'm the mum. I should be able to fix this. I'm the mum!

SCENE TWENTY-FOUR

POPPY: Cleaned out.

Everything shoved away

out of sight

to make it look like good people live here.

[tic, tic]

— Who are you trying to fool?

POPPY: My room

A perfectly clean space for a perfectly perfect girl

[tic]

— Not for you
— twitch twitch
POPPY: Get away from this house
    back down the street
    past a face
— twitch twitch
POPPY: behind the curtain.
    [tic]
    Avoid the village
    avoid the cracks
— Go the back way
— back back back
POPPY: Until
— knock knock knock
LUCY: What do you want?
POPPY: Mrs Porter.
    [tic]
LUCY: What?
POPPY: I … er …
    [tic, tic]
LUCY: Sasha's not here and I wouldn't let her see you if she was.
POPPY: I–I–I'm not here for Sasha. I'm here for you.
LUCY: For what?
POPPY: I want you to take it back.
    [tic]
LUCY: Take what back?
POPPY: What you said to my mum.
LUCY: You're the one who should be taking things back.
POPPY: Tell her you didn't mean it.
LUCY: I meant every word.
POPPY: Call her and tell her.
LUCY: I will do no such thing.
POPPY: Take it back.
    [tic, tic]
LUCY: No.
POPPY: Tell her it's not her fault.
    [tic, tic, tic]
    Tell her!

SASHA: [*offstage*] Poppy? Is that you?

POPPY: I knew she was here.

SASHA: [*offstage*] Poppy! I'm up here.

POPPY: [*to* SASHA] Sasha, I need to talk to you—

LUCY: You keep quiet.

POPPY: [*to* SASHA] I know what did this to us.

LUCY: Go away. She doesn't want to see you.

POPPY: [*to* SASHA] Sasha, are you listening?

SASHA: [*offstage*] I can hear you.

LUCY: [*to* SASHA] She has nothing to say to us, darling. Remember what we talked about …

POPPY: [*to* SASHA] I'm gonna go on TV and—

LUCY: Are you out of your mind?

POPPY: [*to* SASHA] Come with me!

    [tic, tic]

SASHA: [*offstage*] I don't know … I … what should I do?

LUCY: [*to* SASHA] You do as you're told.

POPPY: [*to* SASHA] Sash?

SASHA: [*offstage*] Just do what she says … You don't know what she's like …

POPPY: No … no … I'm coming in—

LUCY: I'll call the police.

POPPY: Who are they going to arrest?

    [tic, tic, tic]

LUCY: I will not let a girl like you ruin my daughter's life.

POPPY: You can't just—

LUCY: It's not your mother's fault.

POPPY: Finally—

LUCY: You're the one who made Sasha sick. It's your fault.

POPPY: No!

LUCY: Your fault it's all over school. Let loose in the hallways—

POPPY: No, that's—

LUCY: Your fault I've had to strap her to the bed.

POPPY: You've what?

    [tic, tic, tic]

LUCY: It's for her own safety.

POPPY: You've got to be kidding—

LUCY: Why hasn't your mother done that to you?

POPPY: I've done nothing wrong.

LUCY: Liar.

POPPY: I am not.

LUCY: Admit it. Go on. Then we can all just move on with our lives.

POPPY: I have nothing to—

LUCY: Admit you made it all up—

POPPY: Seriously?

  [tic, tic]

LUCY: You invented this whole thing—

POPPY: Oh my god—

LUCY: and pulled all your followers along behind you.

POPPY: You mean like your stupid prayers? Are you going to admit you made that shit up?

LUCY: How dare you? You little witch.

POPPY: What?

  [tic, tic]

LUCY: Nobody wants you round here.

POPPY: Sasha is my—

LUCY: Get off my doorstep.

POPPY: No. I–I—

  [tic, tic, tic]

LUCY: Get away from us.

POPPY: Sasha!

SASHA: [*offstage*] What's going on?!

POPPY: I—I—I—I—

    POPPY *'s tics explode.*

SASHA: [*offstage*] Poppy, do what she says, okay? Please! I'm scared!

LUCY: Hear that? She's scared of you.

  I told you, you have no friends here.

    POPPY *takes a step back.*

  Now leave us alone.

SCENE TWENTY-FIVE

POPPY *under bright lights.* SKY *in darkness. A* REPORTER.

POPPY: I think it was there
   somewhere inside—
   at least some nano part of it
   a flicker
   but not—
   [tic]
   Shit.
   Sorry
   [tic, tic, tic]
   When you're a kid and you—

     She blows short bursts through her nose.

   That was me.
   Now
   it's like sparks going off
   and I can't put them out.
REPORTER: You must feel … what? … Trapped almost? Tied within
   your own—
POPPY: No! Actually … no … that's not …
REPORTER: I'm sorry?
POPPY: The truth … the truth is …
REPORTER: Yes?
POPPY: —
   [tic, tic, tic, tic]
   It's not real.
REPORTER: What do you mean?
POPPY: I made it up.
SKY: What?! Poppy?!
POPPY: …
   I mean
   I think it was there
   a flicker
   or—
REPORTER: Why would you do that?
POPPY: I—I—I—
REPORTER: And how do you explain the other girls? Twelve now,
   all from your school. Other schools refusing to play you at sport.

All fixtures cancelled. The evidence, the toxic waste. How do you explain all that?

POPPY: I don't know why the others have it …

Ask them.

[tic, blink, blink]

You'll have to ask them.

REPORTER: One of your friends is right here. Let's ask her. Sky?

> *Bright light now on* SKY *too.*

You're close friends with Poppy.

SKY: … Yes.

REPORTER: And yet you don't have any of these symptoms, do you?

SKY: No. No, I don't.

REPORTER: How do you explain that?

SKY: I don't know. I can't.

REPORTER: And are you worried you're going to get this illness?

SKY: I guess I might.

REPORTER: Do you think you're going to catch it off Poppy?

SKY: No.

REPORTER: So you're saying it must be from somewhere else.

SKY: Well, it's the school's fault … isn't it, Poppy? I'm confused … I thought we were supposed to—

POPPY: She doesn't know what she's talking about.

REPORTER: Where are the other girls? Why didn't they come on the show?

SKY: Their parents won't let them.

REPORTER: Why not?

SKY: Our friend's mum strapped her to the—

POPPY: Sky, stop!

[tic, tic, tic]

REPORTER: Poppy, I have to ask this question. If you made this whole thing up, why don't you just stop now?

POPPY: I—I—I—

[tic, tic, tic]

REPORTER: Can you stop?

POPPY: Nuh nuh nuh—

[tic, tic]

REPORTER: Have you been asked to come on the show today and say what you've said to protect the school?

POPPY: No—I—I—

[tic, tic, tic, tic]

I told you, I made it up.

REPORTER: Are you telling the truth now?

POPPY: I told you.

REPORTER: And … that's all we've got time for.

Bright lights cut off.

Okay. Thanks. That was great.

SKY: How did I look?

REPORTER: Tune in at six, see for yourself.

SCENE TWENTY-SIX

Sheila's office.

SHEILA: Good to see you, Poppy.

POPPY: Nuh nuh nuh …

SHEILA: I see you've been getting into a bit of trouble.

POPPY: Can't hold me down.

[tic, tic]

SHEILA: I have a statement here that says you threatened Mrs Porter. What's that about?

POPPY: —

[tic, tic, tic]

Did you see me on TV?

SHEILA: Yes.

POPPY: I told them I made it up.

SHEILA: I saw that.

POPPY: They didn't believe me.

SHEILA: People only believe what they want to.

POPPY: Do you believe me?

[tic, tic]

SHEILA: Would it help?

POPPY: You're the expert. I should have told them—

[tic, tic]

You said it first.

SHEILA: That's not exactly what I said.

POPPY: If you agree I made it up—nuh nuh nuh—then that means the
others are all making it up too.

[tic, tic]

SHEILA: No, it doesn't work like that.

POPPY: What?

SHEILA: It's more complicated.

POPPY: So I'm the only one in trouble.

Jesus.

Why did I come here?

SHEILA: Because Mrs Porter will press charges if you don't.

POPPY: Keep you in business for—nuh nuh nuh—years.

SHEILA: On the upside, she's going to start paying the bills. Says it's
her Christian duty.

POPPY: Almost makes me want to stay.

SHEILA: What do you mean?

POPPY: We're leaving town.

[tic, tic]

Me and Mum.

SHEILA: Where are you going?

POPPY: I don't know. Anywhere that's not here.

SHEILA: I'll have to tell Mrs Porter.

POPPY: Go ahead. I'm sure everyone will be happy to be—nuh nuh
nuh—rid of me.

SHEILA: I don't want to be rid of you. I want to help you.

POPPY: Bullshit. You just want something interesting to play with.

SHEILA: Your case is interesting, of course it is.

POPPY: Wake you up from your boring-arse life.

SHEILA: But I care about you too.

POPPY: Too bad.

[tic, tic, tic]

The case is leaving. It's over.

SCENE TWENTY-SEVEN

Poppy's house. The 'For Sale' is sign coming down.

HEATHER: The agent pulled the sale. Everyone she called thinks the
place is toxic. They won't even come to inspect it. She said it's

like trying to sell a serial killer's house, except with all the bodies still in the basement.

POPPY: She actually said that?

HEATHER: It was pretty graphic.

POPPY: So what do we do next?

HEATHER: There's nothing we can do.

POPPY: What about the clean start? Reinvent ourselves?

HEATHER: We can't.

POPPY: Nuh nuh nuh—nuh nuh nuh—

[tic, tic]

HEATHER: I'm sorry.

POPPY: What are we—?

[tic, tic]

What are we going to do?

HEATHER: Stay here … go back to how we were … just be the same, I guess.

POPPY: Nothing's the same.

HEATHER: No …

Pause.

POPPY: It would be better if I wasn't here.

HEATHER: Poppy, no.

POPPY: It would. I ruin everything.

HEATHER: Stop it. I don't ever want to hear you talk like that. You understand?

POPPY: You said everything would be fine.

HEATHER: I know—

POPPY: You were just pretending.

HEATHER: That's what people do … that's what we tell ourselves to get through life. And then we start to believe it … or hope for it at least … and sometimes it is, you know, sometimes it is fine …

POPPY: It's a lie.

HEATHER: It's the only way anybody ever survives.

POPPY: Well, they all know it now anyway.

HEATHER: Who?

POPPY: Everyone. Everyone knows everything is a lie.

HEATHER: What are you talking about?

POPPY: I went on the TV and told them—I made it all up.

HEATHER: What?!

POPPY: All of it. The illness. The tics. The whole crazy—

HEATHER: Why would you say that?

POPPY: Because maybe I did, Heather. Maybe I did make it up.

HEATHER: No. That's not … you fainted … the blinking … we did all those tests—

POPPY: How do you know I wasn't pretending?

HEATHER: The doctors would have known.

POPPY: Are you sure?

HEATHER: I would have known.

POPPY: Would you?

SCENE TWENTY-EIGHT

In the dress shop.

SHOP GIRL: Got the receipt?

POPPY: Nuh nuh nuh. No.

SHOP GIRL: Bad timing. All that stock's just rolled over. Winter season now. Can't do nuthin' without a receipt anyhow.

POPPY: Nuh nuh nuh. Don't want the money.

SHOP GIRL: Hang on. I know you.

POPPY: No.

SHOP GIRL: Yeah, I remember you. You're that girl with the disease. The fainting thing.

POPPY: The TV news. That's where you know me from.

SHOP GIRL: Don't have a TV. So old school.

POPPY: You don't know me then.

SHOP GIRL: I do. You came in the shop.

POPPY: Oh?

[tic]

SHOP GIRL: It was that really hot day I remember 'cause I was like nearly dying I think the aircon was broken or something and I thought I was going to faint then suddenly you were lying on the floor and I was like oh shit someone has actually fainted now and I'm going to have to file a report because of the aircon but you were like jumping up and practically running out the door.

POPPY: You remember that day?

SHOP GIRL: Nothing happens here.

POPPY: Okay, well …

[tic, tic]

I just want you to take this back.

[tic, tic, tic]

SHOP GIRL: But you don't have the receipt.

POPPY: No.

[tic, tic]

SHOP GIRL: And anyway that can't be right because I definitely remember you didn't buy anything, you didn't even try anything on which was strange because normally the change rooms are the hottest when the aircon goes and that's when all the older ladies are like oh, my hot flushes! I just can't seem to breathe!

POPPY: I didn't buy the dress.

SHOP GIRL: What?

POPPY: That's why I want to give it back.

[tic, tic]

SHOP GIRL: You're giving back a dress you didn't buy.

Ohmygod. You're giving back a dress you didn't buy! What? Why?

POPPY: It's killing me.

[tic]

I don't even like dresses. I don't like silk. I thought I deserved it.

[tic, tic]

Look what it's done to me.

SHOP GIRL: You got sick.

POPPY: Yes.

SHOP GIRL: And you're blaming the dress?

POPPY: —

[tic]

I don't want it anymore. You have to take it back.

SHOP GIRL: This is a really nice dress.

POPPY: I don't know what else to do.

SHOP GIRL: What about?

POPPY: All this stuff that's happening to me, I think—

[tic, tic]

I think it was inside me before, I think that's where it began. But

now it's on the outside there's this big space left. I'm scared ... I
don't even know if I'm really a person in there.

SHOP GIRL: Who does?

POPPY: I want to fill the space with something true, something
special, but I don't know where to get it from.
[tic, tic]
Where does that stuff come from?

SHOP GIRL: The sales rack?

> POPPY *struggles to keep back tears. She holds out the dress.*

POPPY: Can you please take this off me?

SHOP GIRL: No.

POPPY: Why not?

SHOP GIRL: I told you. That stock's rolled over.

POPPY: So?

SHOP GIRL: So I can't put it back on the rack. Can't call it a return
without a receipt. And if I knew you stole something I'd have to
call the police.
Wouldn't I?

POPPY: Go on then. Call the police.

SHOP GIRL: Then again ...

POPPY: What?

SHOP GIRL: I do hate filling out forms.

POPPY: But what I did—

SHOP GIRL: Total inconvenience. Really makes the day drag. Plus I'm
sure they'd find a way to blame me.
Anyway, I wouldn't worry too much about that dress. Looks nice
but it was made in a sweatshop in India. It'll fall apart first time
you wash it. That's why they say 'Dry-Clean Only'. Makes it feel
more special.

POPPY: You're as bad as the rest of them.

> SHOP GIRL *takes a second.*

SHOP GIRL: Shit.

POPPY: What?

SHOP GIRL: I just remembered. I actually did see you on the news last
night. They put the clip up online. With you saying how you made
everything up.

POPPY: Oh … Did it look okay?
SHOP GIRL: Oh, yeah. Yeah. Except …
POPPY: What?
SHOP GIRL: Don't read the comments.

SCENE TWENTY-NINE

— Snap snap snap
— Snap snap snap like that
— Achy sort of
— Achy itchy tingling scratch
— Scratch scratch scratch scratch
— Can't see can't ignore
— It's right there
— Here
— Howling at me
— Snap like a scratch
— Tingle
— Snap snap snap snap snap snap snap
— Empty like a
— Energy like a
— Arm slash neck slash throat
— They can hear me

SCENE THIRTY

Playing fields, POPPY *and* SKY. *The others watch on.* POPPY *has the dress.*

POPPY: Sky. Hey.
— Snap snap snap
POPPY: I brought you something. Nuh nuh nuh. Didn't wrap it up
    but …
SKY: It's not Christmas.
POPPY: It just doesn't—nuh nuh nuh—look that good on me.
SKY: You're giving me a second-hand dress?
POPPY: Still got the tags so it's not sweaty or anything.
— Achy tingly not the
SKY: When did you get this?

POPPY: It's the one I got for Sasha's.

[tic]

SKY: Thought your mum wouldn't give you any money.

POPPY: You can wear it for your party. Last chance to get everyone
together before you go. We could do it at my house but I don't
know if anyone will come—nuh nuh nuh—what with everything.
What about your place?

SKY: Not going to be a party. Not at mine. Not at yours.

POPPY: You're just going to disappear? Not even say goodbye?

[tic]

SKY: I'm not going.

— Throat slash arm slash

— Roaring scratching

— Roaring in my

POPPY: Oh. My. God. You failed the test.

SKY: Did not.

POPPY: What?

SKY: I passed the test.

POPPY: And …?

SKY: Failed the interview. Thanks to you making me look like a total
dick on TV and a dud report from evil old Holt. They don't want
me.

POPPY: They don't want you.

[tic]

You.

SKY: Dad's on the warpath. Mum won't stop crying. I've been
grounded basically forever. I'm not even supposed to be talking to
you.

POPPY: They don't want you.

— Scratch scratch

— Look don't look

SKY: Mum's forbidden it.

— Noise coming at me

POPPY: So she blames me now too.

SKY: She says you're a bad influence.

POPPY: I suppose you're made of rainbow unicorn poo?

SKY: You think you're so clever.

— Looking at me

— Scratching at me

— Roaring at me

POPPY: I—

SKY: You made this happen. You've taken over.

POPPY: I didn't mean to.

SKY: You won.

POPPY: Won what?

— Howling at me

— Snap snap snap

SKY: I—I—I—I—

POPPY: What did I win? Sky?

SKY: Not.

> SKY *does the blinking tic.*

Not.

POPPY: What are you doing with your eyes?

— Snap snap snap snap

> SKY *does the blinking tic.*

POPPY: Stop that. It's not funny.

SKY: I don't want your dress.

> SKY *does the blinking tic.*

Give it to I—I—I—someone else.

POPPY: I don't have anyone else.

SKY: I—I—I—I'm not talking to you now. They'll find out.

> SKY *does the blinking tic.*

POPPY: Come on. It's just me. Stop mucking about.

SKY: I have to—

Nuh nuh nuh nuh—

I have to go.

POPPY: Sky?

Sky!

> *All the other girls are there, ticc-ing around the edges. They may never go away.*

THE END

THE UNCERTAINTY PRINCIPLE AND THE OLD 505 THEATRE

present

NORMAL

29 MAY—15 JUNE 2019

Writer
Katie Pollock

Director
Anthony Skuse

Assistant director
Olivia Aleksoski

Light and set designer
Kelsey Lee

Sound designer
Cluny Edwards

Stage manager
Gundega Lapsa

Assistant producer
James Balian

With

Shop girl/Ms Holt/Lucy/ensemble **– Chika Ikogwe**
Poppy **– Alexandra Morgan**
Heather/Sasha/ensemble **– Cecilia Morrow**
Sky/Sheila/ensemble **– Finley Penrose**

the
uncertainty
principle

THE OLD 505 THEATRE

DIRECTOR'S NOTE

She: I have heard it said / There is great danger in the body.

W.B. Yeats, Michael Robartes and the Dancer, *1921*

Working on Katie Pollock's *Normal* has made me hyper aware that women's bodies are as often the site of their own rebellion, as they are the locus of male anxiety. I think of the medieval mystics who starved themselves, the Jacobean heroines such as Beatrice-Joanna and Vittoria Corombona whose bodies were under constant siege, linguistically and dramatically, of the under-represented young women in Arthur Miller's *The Crucible*.

Each character in Pollock's play struggles with the social and cultural expectations placed upon them. Each of these women are negotiating a patriarchal structure that allows them little agency and no real power. I think of women in Gothic literature, which first appeared in the mid-eighteenth century, who are either powerful and malevolent forces or innocent victims.

For all these women the very notion of normal is a thin membrane that has been stretched over their daily existence. And in each case, they are compelled to rupture it, if they want to breath freely. The Gothic genre is a useful lens through which to view Pollock's play, with its isolated protagonist caught in a landscape weaponized by unspoken or sublimated fears. I think of Joan Lindsay's *Picnic at Hanging Rock*, where the one girl who does come back from the rock is shunned because of what she has seen. After such knowledge, what forgiveness?[1] By the end of *Normal*, Poppy finds herself to be as terrifyingly alone.

—**Anthony Skuse**

[1] T.S. Eliot, *Gerontion*, 1920

KATIE POLLOCK
PLAYWRIGHT

Katie's plays for theatre are *The Becoming* (Redline Productions; New Theatre); *The Hansard Monologues—Age of Entitlement* (Seymour Centre/ Merrigong Theatre/Glen Street Theatre/Museum of Australian Democracy); *Blue Italian/Nil by Sea* (Site & Sound Festival); *The Hansard Monologues—A Matter of Public Importance* (Seymour Centre/ Merrigong Theatre/Casula Powerhouse/Museum of Australian Democracy); *The Blue Angel Hotel* (Old Fitzroy); *A Quiet Night in Rangoon* (subtlenuance/ New Theatre); *A Girl Called Red* (Newtown Theatre); and numerous short works.

Katie's plays and adaptations for radio are *Beetroot: A bloody journey through roots and belonging* (ABC Radio National); *Nil by Sea* (ABC Radio National); *Contact* (Eastside FM); *Basketcase* (Eastside FM) *O is for Oxygen* (ABC Radio National); and *Blue Italian* (ABC Radio National).

Katie is the winner of the Rodney Seaborn Playwrights Award for *People Inside Me*; the Martin Lysicrates Prize for *Summerland*; the inaugural Town Hall Theatre (USA) 'Ingenious' grant, the Inscription/Edward Albee Playwriting Scholarship and the Australian Writers' Guild's What Happens Next competition for *Normal*; and Hothouse Theatre's Solo competition for *Contact*. She has been nominated for two AWGIES and has been a finalist in two Silver Gull Awards, the Woodward/Newman Drama Award (USA), and the Leah Ryan FEWW Playwrights Prize (USA).

ANTHONY SKUSE
DIRECTOR

Anthony's directing credits include: *Crime and Punishment* (Secret House); *The Street of Crocodiles* (AFTT, Belvoir Downstairs); *Air* (Old 505); *The Seagull* (Secret House); *Play Without a Title* (AFTT, Belvoir Downstairs); *Birdland* (New Theatre); *4.48 Psychosis* (Old Fitz); *Herons* (ISA); *Sunset Strip* (Uncertainty Principle, Griffin); *Between the Streetlight and the Moon* (Mophead Productions); *Mystery of Love and Sex* (Darlinghurst Theatre); *Airswimming* (The Vaults, London); *Our Class* (AFTT, Belvoir Downstairs); *Man With Five Children* (Darlinghurst Theatre); *Dropped* (Old Fitz); *Blood Bank* (Ensemble); *Fourplay & Ride* (Darlinghurst Theatre); *The House of Ramon Iglesia* (Mophead Productions); *Caress/Ache* (Griffin); *Shabbat Dinner* (Rock Surfers, Rocks Pop Up Festival, Griffin); *Platonov* (ATYP Selects); *Constellations* (Darlinghurst Theatre); *Stop Kiss* (Unlikely Productions); *Bite Me* (ATYP); *On the shore of the wide world* (Griffin Independent); *4000 Miles* (Under the Wharf, Sydney & La Boite, Brisbane); *Punk Rock* (Under the Wharf—three Sydney Theatre Awards including Best Independent Production and Best Direction); *Dioclesian* (Pinchgut Opera); *Bug*, *References to Salvador Dali Make Me Hot*, *The Cold Child*, *Live Acts On Stage* (Griffin Independent); *pool (no water)*, and *Terrorism* (Darlinghurst Theatre).

Anthony is Head of Performance at Actors Centre Australia. He was Associate Lecturer for Performance Practices at NIDA from 2009 to 2012.

Training: Drama Studio Sydney. In 1997 and 2001 he worked with Javanese Movement Practitioner Suprapto Suryodarmo.

OLIVIA ALEKSOSKI
ASSISTANT DIRECTOR

Olivia Aleksoski is a 2017 graduate of the Actors Centre Australia (ACA). She is currently shooting her first short film *Her Own Music* that she has written, and will also direct. She was recently assistant director on *Fierce* (The Old Fitz). Directing credits include: *It Doesn't Snow Here* (Sydney Fringe); *Anyone Can Whistle* (King St Theatre); *The Hatpin* (assistant director, Blue Elephant theatre, London). As an actor she has appeared in *UBU* (NIDA); *The Boys* dir. Angela Punch-McGregor, *Romeo and Juliet* dir. Adam Cook. *Transience*, dir. Anthony Skuse and Julia Cotton. She's excited to be working with Anthony Skuse again on *Wink* at KXT later this year as asisstant director and stage manager.

KELSEY LEE
LIGHT AND SET DESIGNER

Kelsey is a set, lighting and costume designer for theatre and film. She most recently designed the lighting for *Extinction of The Learned Response* (Belvoir 25A); set, lighting and costume for *There's A Sea In My Bedroom* (ACO); lighting for *Fierce* (Redline Productions); set and lighting for *Comedy Kiki* (Darlinghurst Theatre Company); lighting for *If We Got Some More Cocaine I Could Show You How I Love You* (KXT) and *The Other Side Of 25* (Old 505). Previous work includes set, lighting and costume for *LULU: A Modern Sex Tragedy* (NIDA); lighting for *The Humans* (Redline/ Mophead Productions); co-design for *Shabbat Dinner* (Griffin); set and costumes for *AIR* (Old 505); costume assistant for *Stupid Fucking Bird* (New Theatre); production design for web series *Your Mates*; production design for *C'mon: Lleyton Hewitt The Musical* (ATYP); assistant set, lighting and costume design on *Spring Awakening* (ATYP). She completed an internship with Fox Studios for the film *Ladies In Black* and has worked extensively across departments at Belvoir St, Griffin, Ensemble and Opera Australia.

CLUNY EDWARDS
SOUND DESIGNER

Cluny studied Music and Drama at the Arts Educational School in London. He played in various bands in the UK, where he had a publishing and recording contract as a singer/songwriter. He later established a recording studio in France, where he wrote and produced music for advertising, theatre and film. He composed *Ni Ange Ni Bete*, a musical performed at the Casino de Paris in association with the French Aids Association and *Jerusalem* a musical performed at the Sadie Bronfman Centre, Montreal, Canada. Cluny has also written and produced advertising soundtracks for Ford Europe, Radio France and Heli-Air Monaco. After moving to Australia he has continued to work on an eclectic mix of projects, including previous plays by Katie Pollock *The Blue Angel Hotel* (Old Fitzroy Theatre) and *Contact* (Eastside FM).

GUNDEGA LAPSA
STAGE MANAGER

Gundega graduated from the University of London with a Bachelor of Arts in Philosophy, Religion and Ethics. Currently she is the assistant director for *Pygmalion*, Dir. Deborah Mulhall (New Theatre) and production manager for *Table*, Dir. Kim Hardwick (White Box Theatre, Seymour Centre). Gundega has also worked as the production manager for *What the Butler Saw*, Dir. Danielle Mass (New Theatre), stage manager for *The Lieutenant of Inishmore*, Dir. Deborah Mulhall (New Theatre) and *Plenty Serious Talk Talk*, Dir. Vicki Van Hout, (Form Dance Projects and Riverside Theatre).

JAMES BALIAN
ASSISTANT PRODUCER

James' previous writing credits include the play *The Night After the Day Before* (Ensemble Studios), the telemovie *Thank You Jack* (ABC), and the tele-play *An Electric Day* (ABC). James wrote and directed the feature film *Saturday Night* (SBS, Cinequest Film Festival). He has written and directed many productions for Short and Sweet and was Gala finalist in 2010 and 2011. He wrote and directed *The Viagra Monologues* and *The New Deal* (Sydney Fringe Festival). In 2014 he produced his play *Brother Daniel* at the Tap Gallery. In 2016 he produced *A Nest of Skunks* at the Depot Theatre, which he co-wrote with Roger Vickery. In July 2018 his work featured in the Raw Bites Road-Trip Monologues show in Los Angeles (https://outlook.live.com/owa/projection.aspx). His most recent play was *Mum, Me and the IED*, co-written with Roger Vickery and directed by Kevin Jackson (Depot Theatre).

CHIKA IKOGWE
SHOP GIRL / MS HOLT / LUCY / ENSEMBLE

Chika Ikogwe is a Nigerian-Australian actor, writer and recent acting graduate of NIDA. Before NIDA, Chika studied at the VCA, in the Bachelor of Fine Arts (Theatre Practice) course. Her screen credits include *I Gotta Have You* performed by Fluir, and the webseries *All We Have Is Now*. Her theatre credits include *All That Glitters*, *Salem*, *The Country Wife*, *The Colby Sisters of Pittsburgh Pennsylvania*, *Women on the Verge of a Nervous Breakdown* (NIDA). Chika made her professional theatre in *The Wolves* (Belvoir). She received the 2018 BBM Youth Support Award in Drama, was a finalist in the 2018 *Home and Away* Internship 2018 and received the Leslie Walford AM Award in 2019. She was co-writer on the award winning web series *Afrosistahs* and co-writer on *The House at Boundary Road Liverpool,* which will premiere at The Old 505 Theatre in November 2019.

ALEXANDRA MORGAN
POPPY

Alexandra gradulated from Actors Centre Australia in 2017 and before that NIDA's Screen Actors Studio in 2014. While at Actors Centre, Alexandra appeared in *Hamlet*, *The Importance of Being Ernest* and *Children of The Sun*. Since graduating, her credits include the series pilot *Your Mates*, *The Bacchae* (NIDA, Adelaide Fringe Festival) and *Whose Uterus Is It Anyway?* (Old 505Theatre). She also just produced and starred in the short film *Her Own Music*. Alexandra is driven to create works that tell stories about multi-dimensional women.

CECILIA MORROW
HEATHER/SASHA/ENSEMBLE

Cecilia is a graduate of Actors Centre Australia. Credits include *The Cherry Orchard* (New Theatre), *Crazy Brave* (Cross Pollinate Productions), *The Local* (Insomniact Productions), *Safekeeping* (The New Plot), *The Last Tiger* (The New Plot), *Headcase* (The New Plot), *Amongst Ruins: Snake Eggs Hatch* (New Fitz), *Mercury Fur* (KXT Teethcutting), *The Telescope* (New Fitz), *Home Invasion* (An Assorted Few), *Pramkicker* (Vox Theatre), *Sheilas* (Giant Dwarf/Screen Australia), *Winter* (Channel 7) and *Top of the Lake* (BBC/Sundance TV). Cecilia is a proud Equity member.

FINLEY PENROSE
SKY/SHEILA/ENSEMBLE

As one of Sydney's premiere emerging nonbinary transgender actors, Finley is an artist driven towards work that centres the queer experience, as well as authentic stories that touch upon invisible disability, oppression and the human condition. Born in New York and raised in Hong Kong, Finn has been privileged to work with many inter-cultural artistic practices and has been involved in a diverse range of productions including the Hong Kong Youth Arts Foundation's *Ms Directing*—a celebration of female and gender-ambiguous Shakespearean characters. *Normal* marks their second time to grace the Old 505's stage after appearing in Georgina Adamson's *Whose Uterus Is it Anyway?* as part of FreshworksFEMME in November 2018.

WITH THANKS

The author gratefully acknowledges the support of the Australia Council, the Australian Writers' Guild, Inscription, Town Hall Theatre, WITS, Kerri Glassock and the team at The Old 505 Theatre, and all of the people who have been part of the journey of this play, including:

Nick Atkins, Madeleine Baghurst, Rowan Bate, Kate Bookalil, Rachel Chant, Fraser Corfield, Timothy Daly, Benito DiFonzo, Katrina Douglas, Timothy Jones, Mark Kilmurry, Poppy Lynch, Sarah Meacham, Jane Phegan, Lachlan Philpott, Jen Rani, Haley Rice, Whitney Richards, Melita Rowston, Katherine Thomson, May Tran, Claudia Ware, Emily Weir, Marcus West and David Williams.

I especially want to thank Anthony Skuse for putting his faith in this play; Peter Fray for his support; and Sarah Christopher, Suzi Dougherty, Merridy Eastman and Suzie Miller for their unwavering friendship, encouragement and advice.

Most of all, thanks to my children, Madigan and Bobby, with all my love.

ABOUT THE UNCERTAINTY PRINCIPLE

Led by Artistic Director Suzie Miller, The Uncertainty Principle is a theatre company established in London UK and Sydney Australia. Aiming for a global dialogue, The Uncertainty Principle creations incorporate either movement as language, site-specific forms, interactive, experiential and engaged immersion culminating in thrilling festival and event theatre—one off small pieces or large scale works—that use bodies, physicality, design, idea generation, visual projection, diversity, music and language in ways that are relevant to contemporary life and speak to a new century theatre audience. Always underpinning any new forms with dynamic and narrative text—we aim to create challenging and relevant work that continues to collaborate with exceptional artists, and other exciting companies.